INTO's
Woman Presidents
1868 – 2025

NOEL WARD

Irish National Teachers' Organisation
Cumann Múinteoirí Éireann

INTO's Woman Presidents 1868-2025

by Noel Ward

Copyright ©2025 Noel Ward

ISBN 978-1-916620-88-9

Published by the Irish National Teachers' Organisation

This edition printed and bound in the Republic of Ireland by

lettertec

Lettertec Publishing

Springhill House,

Carrigtwohill

Co. Cork

Republic of Ireland

www.selfpublishbooks.ie

Contents

Foreword

Is mór an onóir agus pléisiúr dúinn an gné tábhachtach seo do stair CMÉ a bheith tugtha chun solais. Through the lens of the INTO women presidents, we can see the history of our organisation, the education system and society in Ireland reflected.

These women's interests and achievements encompass the themes of INTO's work over the past 157 years. They championed causes including pay equality, employment rights, class size, disadvantage, special and remedial education, school buildings and small schools. They were involved in the wider education eco-system, representing their colleagues on bodies such as commissions for education, the Teaching Council and the National Council for Curriculum and Assessment (NCCA). Many were also active in trades councils and the Irish Congress of Trade Unions.

The INTO women presidents were active and engaged in many aspects of Irish life. Their energy and commitment to their chosen causes radiates off the pages. There are many interesting stories touched on, including participation in struggles for Irish independence and women's suffrage, a trip to the Philippines, involvement with the 1946 and 1985 strikes, the beginnings of the INTO Separated Teachers' Support and LGBTQ+ groups, and an All-Ireland Ladies Football medal. These activities underline how teachers and the INTO are woven into the fabric of Irish life.

Further progress in gender equality can never be taken for granted. Catherine Mahon was elected president in 1912, at a time when many Irish women were politically engaged and hopeful that the independent country they fought for would grant them freedom and equality. For many of these women, that aspiration was not fulfilled, and it took INTO over thirty years to elect another woman president. There have now been eleven women presidents since the turn of this century, and they belonged to INTO central executive committees (CECs) which were more gender-balanced and with a woman general secretary (the first elected to any union in Ireland) or deputy general secretary/general treasurer for most of those years. The current CEC has a woman president, vice-president, and ex-president. Women officials have been in the majority in the same period, while women have always been the backbone of the workforce in head office and Northern office.

However, in today's world, we cannot be complacent about gender equality or women's place in our society. As a union and a profession where more than 80 per cent are female, the example of these presidents' visiting schools and branches as leaders of the union cannot be underestimated. The stories of these women remind us of the importance of strong women and their right to be in every space.

Táimid íontach buíoch do Noel Ward as an leabhar taitneamhach tairbheach seo a scríobh - leabhar a chuidíonn linn ceiliúradh a dhéanamh ar an ról tábhachtach a d'imir na mná a toghadh mar uachtaráin ar Chumann Múinteoirí Éireann go dtí seo.

John Boyle, General Secretary
Deirdre O'Connor, Deputy General Secretary/ General Treasurer

Introduction

This publication recalls and recognises twenty women who, over the past 113 years, have been elected as president of the Irish National Teachers' Organisation (INTO), and the current president-elect who at Easter 2025 is to become the 21st female president.

Why Focus on Woman Presidents?

Until quite recently, women in the INTO presidency were a rarity. Having reached twenty in number, it is timely to recall each of those who accepted the challenge of this office.

While conscious of current discourse around gender identity, diversity and fluidity, an examination of female leadership within a union with INTO's make-up remains a project of relevance and worth.

Woman presidents up to and including the 1980s worked with INTO executive committees which were heavily male-dominated. These presidents were often the lone female present at the central executive committee (CEC) table. The more recent female presidents have, like their predecessors, been a visible reminder to INTO's women members of those members' potential to lead the organisation. Each has rendered a service in terms of the aphorism 'If you can't see it, you can't be it'.

The male presidents also merit recognition but the focus here is on the women. Historically, they have taken a road less travelled and to highlight them is not to downplay the contribution of others.

INTO Presidents: Gender and Other Factors

Since its foundation in 1868, the INTO has chosen a president each year. Among the president's current roles are representing the union at home and abroad, acting alongside the general secretary as a spokesperson, and chairing significant meetings including those of the CEC, of other regular events (such as the yearly Education Conference), and of INTO Annual Congress.

The earlier woman presidents were pioneers in the field of seeking female representation in INTO's leadership while those elected more recently have been part of a progression towards reflecting more closely the gender composition of the membership.

Women teachers have formed most of that membership for more than a century. The union's journal reported that in 1908 there were 5,740 male, and 7,395 female, national teachers (*Irish School Weekly*, 20 January 1912, p.1250). The female majority has increased substantially since then. The 21,863 women teachers made up 83 per cent of the total employed (Republic of Ireland only) twenty years ago (*INTO Central Executive Committee Report* 2005-2006, p.103) and that proportion is little different today.

Election of a larger number of woman presidents has been a recent feature of INTO history. To illustrate this, when her biography of INTO's first woman president Catherine Mahon was published, Síle Chuinneagáin observed that 'in the 90 years since Mahon was first elected to the Executive there have been only nine women Presidents' (Chuinneagáin 1998, p.220). We now know that, in the twenty-seven years since that book was published, there have been a further eleven women chosen as president.

The term of office of an INTO president is one year. Most have served, prior to election to the presidency, in the office of district representative on INTO's CEC and as vice president. Neither that service nor the one-year term have applied to all presidents, however. A total of thirteen men have held the office for more than one year. The union's first president, Vere

Foster, served for five years. The record in terms of longevity is Tipperary's John Nealon's seven years in the role between 1883 and 1906. In the 20th century two non-sequential terms were served by each of five male presidents, including Denis Maher, Tom Nunan, Cormac Breathnach and Tom Frisby. The fifth, George O'Callaghan, was president in 1911-1912 and again from 1914 to 1916 (as there was no Annual Congress held in 1915). Among the women, only Catherine Mahon has held the office for more than one year, serving two successive terms from 1912 to 1914.

A grandfather and granddaughter (Tom and Sheila Nunan) have served in the INTO presidency as have a father and son (Eamonn and Joseph Mansfield). One school in Ballina, Co Mayo, has seen four presidents work there – DF (Frank) Courell, Liam Reilly, Frank Cunningham, and Seán Rowley – a record not unrelated to a lengthy dispute about the takeover of that school by a religious order. (For an account of the Ballina dispute, see Puirséil 2017, pp. 128-133).

To summarise the gender profile, there were no woman INTO presidents during the union's first forty-four years (1868-1912). Over the full 157 years (1868–2025) since the founding of the INTO, there have been twenty females, alongside 104 male, presidents.

How INTO compares in respect of female presidents with other major representative, cultural and sporting organisations which have substantial female membership has not been investigated in detail. It is, however, difficult to recall a woman at the head of a number of such bodies.

Woman Presidents in Context

While some woman presidents (especially where elections were contested) stressed their commitment to issues of particular concern to women, all (in common with their male counterparts) served in the office with distinction. Since the success of Róisín Carabine in a contest for the vice presidency in 1984, each of the more recent female presidents has been elected unopposed to both the vice presidency and presidency.

Notwithstanding the predominance of female teachers in INTO's membership, it cannot be assumed that a female candidate will inevitably be victorious in an election. Women who contested the vice presidency in 1980, 1981 and 1990 were unsuccessful. It was undoubtedly a factor that in each case the male candidate elected had a record of service as a CEC district representative to bolster his candidacy.

In approaching the task of writing a pen-picture of each of these woman leaders, I sought to locate their presidency in its wider context. Some of the earlier of these office-holders served at high points of INTO activity: the battle around a harsh inspectorial regime and the dismissal of INTO's vice president (Catherine Mahon's term of office), the protracted salary strike of 1946 (Kathleen Clarke), the 1980s and another major salary dispute (Róisín Carabine). Presidents in office in the period from 1995 to 2007 had terms which coincided with the 'Celtic Tiger' years of rapid economic growth. By contrast, their immediate successors served during a time of severe recession from 2008, with signs of recovery from 2014 although the deleterious effect of cuts from that recession have been felt long after that date.

In addition to biographical information about each female president, mention will be made of some notable features of their term of office. There will be little coverage of the regular, daily work but it may be taken that each participated to a greater or lesser extent in what have become standard activities for such office-holders - rounds of school visits; representing INTO at meetings, seminars, conferences and in negotiations; lobbying of public representatives; addressing training sessions, rallies and protests; attending sporting occasions involving schoolchildren; celebrating teacher retirements; being part of other INTO branch and district events; and some attendance at funerals.

Secondment from teaching duties to work full-time while in office as INTO president accompanies election to the position. We know, however, that Catherine Mahon continued teaching during her two terms as president and that her salary was deducted for some of her absences on deputations

(Chuinneagáin 1998, p.138, and p.152 n.19). It may be inferred - from the fulsome welcome given to the release from school duties afforded to her - that Kathleen Clarke was the first INTO president, female or male, to avail of the now standard leave from teaching duties (*Irish School Weekly*, 14 & 21 July 1945, p.831).

Research augmented by Personal Knowledge

In recognising the subjects of this publication, a decision was made to adopt a broadly similar length (of approximately 500 words) for each individual pen picture. Editorial decisions had to be made in respect of each piece in order to have reasonable consistency of coverage. Two of these presidents have had full-length biographies published, as referenced in the text.

Researching and drafting for this booklet has demonstrated to me how much more difficult it is to write about living persons, presidents whom I know or have known, than to do so in respect of the first six INTO woman presidents who are no longer with us. A serious effort has been made to be descriptive, and neither judgemental nor comparative.

Since I joined the union in 1976 I have met and most often, as a member of the INTO executive committee, have worked with those included below who have served since the 1970s. I succeeded Fiona Poole as district representative in 1988 and later worked as an INTO official, including as deputy general secretary from 2010 to 2021, with several other presidents. For full disclosure, I should add that I am married to my namesake, the tenth woman president listed below.

There are many women who have served or are serving in prominent and important INTO roles, locally and more centrally, who never became president. Among those in the distant past was Rose Timmins, campaigner for lay teachers in religious-community schools and only (from 1918) the second woman to serve on the executive of the Irish Trade Union Congress. Much more recently, they include the skilled and valued colleagues with whom I worked in INTO head office over many years. INTO has had one female general secretary (Sheila Nunan) to date and four women have served as treasurer, the final three of the following list elected to that office and also as deputy general secretary: Mairéad Ashe, Catherine Byrne, Sheila Nunan and Deirdre O'Connor.

Among other women giving valuable service to INTO are staff representatives, branch and district activists, members of national committees, and the women who have served as CEC district representatives without going on to the presidency (see Appendix 3). The particular focus of this publication does not diminish in any way the value of service given to INTO by many women and men not listed here.

A Note on Sources

At the end of this publication there is a list of the main sources consulted. Here is a note on how each has been utilised.

I have relied heavily on INTO journals and other published sources for this work. The *Irish School Weekly* (*ISW*, published from 1904 and explicitly under INTO's editorial control from 1919) was of great value. Successor INTO publications – among them *An Múinteoir Náisiúnta, Tuarascáil* and *InTouch* – were also important resources. Searches of these journals were complemented by a review of relevant press coverage, accessed through the *Irish Newspaper Archive*.

Niamh Puirséil's *Kindling the Flame* (2017), a 150-year history of the INTO, is an indispensable resource and was consulted many times. Each of the presidents up to the mid-1980s has an index reference in this book and the section titled 'Women in the INTO' (pp. 158-161) offers a perspective on male domination up to the late 1970s.

TJ O'Connell's INTO centenary book *100 Years of Progress 1868-1968* was also consulted. O'Connell devoted his chapter five to 'Women Teachers' and highlighted some issues of concern to these members. His photographs include 'the five women presidents' (facing p. 208) and a striking one of the nineteen-member CEC for 1967-1968 (facing p. 225) with just one female, Alice Brennan, who would become INTO's sixth woman president. This latter photograph is reproduced at p.19 below.

I have referred above to Síle Chuinneagáin's biography of Catherine Mahon, an essential source when researching Mahon, the INTO and education in her times. Other relevant biographical works including entries in the *Dictionary of Irish Biography* were also consulted. Certain records were of use in particular contexts; these include the Irish Trade Union Congress (ITUC) annual reports available on the website of the Irish Labour History Society, and the *Historical Directory of Trade Unions in Ireland* (2017), compiled by Francis Devine and John B Smethurst. State records – such as the online census forms from 1901 and 1911 and the website irishgenealogy.ie – were consulted in respect of earlier presidents.

Interviews were not conducted but at a late stage of drafting each president from Fiona Poole (president 1978-1979) to Carmel Browne (2024-2025) inclusive – and president-elect for 2025-2026 Anne Horan – was sent a draft of material compiled about them. Each was offered an opportunity to comment, particularly where there may have been inaccuracies or omissions of important events during a presidency. The responses received following this stage were helpful in completing the final text.

Acknowledgements

This publication originated in a conversation with Carmel Browne at INTO's Killarney Congress in 2023 as she assumed the vice-presidential office. We discussed whether she was the first Roscommon native, and/or the first person teaching in Longford, to be so elected. I undertook to investigate this and in so doing realised that she would likely be the 20th woman president of INTO, which she became at Easter 2024. Our conversation had planted the seed.

At an early stage I advised general secretary John Boyle and deputy general secretary Deirdre O'Connor about this project. Both have been encouraging and helpful throughout. Mentioning others from INTO head office who have assisted runs the risk of omitting a person or persons on whom I have relied but I must nonetheless thank some people particularly. David Donnelly has been unfailingly helpful as have Georgina Glackin, Ann McConnell, Ruth Warren, Christine Collins, Karen Francis, Selina Campbell and Jeanne Sutton. My thanks also to former president Seán Rowley who sourced locally information about the later years of the life of Kathleen Clarke.

A late draft of this publication was reviewed critically by Dr Eilís O'Sullivan whose observations were greatly appreciated and have influenced its final shape. The portrait photographs are from INTO files: Moya Nolan has taken these for many years and to her goes the credit for them and for several of the other, more modern, photographs. Earlier photographs were sourced almost exclusively in INTO publications, an exception being that of Catherine Mahon at Carrig National School, an image contained in Síle Chuinneagáin's biography and originally provided by Anthony Dargan. Finally, the work of Lettertec - and in particular Jennifer Matthews who managed the project there - in the areas of design, layout and printing was much appreciated.

And so, on the election and during the term of office (2024-2025) of Carmel Browne as INTO's 20th woman president, all twenty (and the 21st as president elect) are recalled as teachers, INTO activists and union representatives.

It will be generally accepted that the election of the next twenty-one INTO woman presidents is unlikely to take anything like a further 157 years.

Noel Ward
January 2025

Three INTO Presidents Meet

Róisín Carabine at a presentation to honour her in her native Belfast at INTO Congress 2017: l to r Rosena Jordan (president 2016-2017), Róisín Carabine (president 1985-1986) and general secretary Sheila Nunan (president 2005-2006).

INTO's
Woman Presidents
1868-2025

Catherine Mahon (1869-1948)
President 1912-1914

Catherine Mahon

For forty-four years until Catherine Mahon's election, all INTO presidents had been males. Born in 1869 and qualifying as a teacher through the monitorial system at the Convent of Mercy NS, Birr, Co Offaly, Mahon's main teaching career was as principal of Carrig NS in north Tipperary. She was a supporter of the Gaelic League and the suffragette movement.

Until 1907 there had never been a woman on INTO's executive (CEC). In that year, while Catherine Mahon had been an unsuccessful candidate for the vice presidency, both she and Elizabeth Larmour were elected to CEC positions newly reserved for 'lady teachers', as principals' representative and assistants teachers' representative, respectively.

As a CEC member, Mahon advocated strongly for equal pay regardless of a teacher's gender, and worked to recruit more women teachers into the union. After four very active years on the INTO executive she was elected unopposed as vice president in 1911 and as INTO's first female president in 1912.

In office, she fought an uncompromising battle to secure reinstatement of INTO vice president Eamonn Mansfield who had been sacked for public criticism of an inspector. She gave striking testimony over four days in 1913 at the Dill Commission which examined oppressive inspection. In 1913 also she was re-elected unopposed for a second presidential term (the only woman to date to have served more than one year in the role).

She had the clear confidence of executive colleagues at a critical time regarding inspection and free speech, as evidenced by a CEC resolution reported in the *Irish School Weekly* in January 1913. This proposed that 'in view of the crisis' facing the Organisation, 'it would be a judicious thing to retain Miss Mahon in her position as President for another year'.

After leaving the executive in 1916 she had public, personalised disagreements with INTO leaders about the union's support for the McPherson Education Bill (1919), resulting in an INTO-sponsored libel action against her. She did not take further active part in the INTO after this episode.

As a delegate from South King's County Trades Council at the 1920 annual meeting of the Irish Labour Party and Trade Union Congress (ILPTUC), Catherine Mahon proposed a radical motion on Agricultural Policy, calling for 'public ownership of all land'. Active in Cumann na mBan during the

War of Independence, she was later awarded a service medal to recognise this but her application for a service pension was unsuccessful.

In the 1930s, having retired from teaching, she was elected for the Fianna Fáil party as the first woman on North Tipperary County Council. An invited guest at INTO Congress in 1946, she spoke impressively in support of the then ongoing salary strike, alongside INTO's second woman president, Kathleen Clarke.

She lived from 1937 with family in Balbriggan, Co Dublin, where she died in 1948 and is buried. Síle Chuinneagáin's book *Catherine Mahon – First Woman President of the INTO* was published by the INTO in 1998. The (online) *Dictionary of Irish Biography* includes an entry on Mahon, written by Bridget Hourican.

Catherine Mahon and pupils at Carrig NS, 1905, two years before her election to the INTO executive.

Kathleen Clarke (1886-1974)
President 1945-1946

Kathleen Clarke

From near Kiltimagh, Co Mayo, Kathleen Clarke (previously Carney) was born in January 1886.

She became a teacher at her local Treenagleragh NS, and won a contested election to the INTO executive from Easter 1935 as the assistant teachers' representative for the western district. She was returned to this position each year to 1944, becoming increasingly conspicuous on senior INTO deputations to Ministers and the Inspectorate. Her husband and teaching colleague Patrick (whom she had married in 1916) was also a prominent INTO member and a branch officer; he died prematurely in 1936.

Kathleen was known locally as 'Katherine' ('Katherine Mary' and 'Catherine' also appear for her on state records) but was 'Kathleen' in INTO publications. She has occasionally been confused with her namesake Kathleen, a noted nationalist and Dublin's first woman Lord Mayor.

In 1938 she addressed a Dublin meeting about discrimination affecting women teachers, saying that 'deep-rooted prejudices against women as women applied also in other professions, and their day is nearly done'. At the 1941 INTO Congress, she proposed a motion demanding withdrawal of the 1938 regulation requiring female teachers to retire at age 60 and the rule which forced the same teachers to retire on marriage. Urging women members to let their voices be heard she declared: 'The days when men must work and women must weep are gone forever'. She led a discussion at Congress 1942 by reading a paper on the position of women teachers.

On issues then very relevant to female colleagues – the Needlework programme and the teaching of Cookery – she prepared policy papers adopted by INTO for submission to the Department.

The only woman on the CEC during this period (1935-1944), she was elected unopposed to the vice presidency in 1944, and as INTO's second woman president in 1945.

Apparently the first president to be released from school duties during her term, she led the union at the outset of the seven-month pay strike by Dublin teachers in 1946. As the strike commenced she wrote that the 'waiting of years has come to a head … the teachers are minded to go no more on their knees'. Listing the categories of teachers to go on strike she declared that 'Desperation has lent them courage'. Her presidential address to the INTO Congress of that year was a further setting out of the striking teachers' case.

After her retirement in 1951, Kathleen Clarke (as 'Kathleen Mary Clarke') was nominated as a Seanad election candidate in both 1952 and 1954 but was unsuccessful.

While little about her later life could be found in INTO or state records, local information from Co Mayo indicates that in retirement Kathleen was active in the Irish Countrywomen's Association and was elected to its national executive. She eventually went to stay at a convent/retirement home at Lough Glynn, Co Roscommon. She died there on 23 December 1974 (*Irish Press*, 24 December 1974). The *Annual Report for 1974-1975* of INTO's CEC recorded her death with 'profound regret', recalling her presidency 'during the turbulent period 1945-1946'.

Kathleen Clarke with members of the INTO executive during the 1946 strike: l to r front row: T.J. O'Connell (general secretary), Kathleen Clarke (president 1945-1946), Dave Kelleher (president 1946-1947), Norah Higgins, Sean McGlinchey. L to r back row: Hugh O'Connor, Pat Carney, Sean Sweeney, TJ Foley, Ignatius H McEnaney.

Bríd Bergin (1892-1976)
President 1950-1951

Bríd Bergin

Kilkenny born, and the first Dublin-based teacher to become president, Bríd (Brighid/Bridget) Bergin, a member of the INTO strike committee in 1946, was one of several strike leaders to contest central leadership positions afterwards. Included in photographs of a final picket at the Department of Education just before the dispute ended, she had been a teacher in North King Street NS and by the early 1930s was principal of St Joseph's School in Dorset Street. Having previously been listed with a BA degree, she was awarded an MA which, from the mid-1930s, was generally appended to her name.

She was elected in 1947 as principals' representative for the eastern district on the CEC, outpolling a male candidate by a narrow margin and saying afterwards that 'women thought that women should represent them on the CEC'. The following year, she unsuccessfully contested the vice presidency, advocating equal pay for men and women, and polling 43 per cent of the vote. Further evidence of her identification with women teachers was her joint letter with another defeated candidate (Margaret Ambrose of Cork) sent to the INTO journal after this election. In 1949, Bríd Bergin won the vice presidency, defeating another Dublin City branch candidate. On the same day, Margaret Skinnider, who was to become the fourth woman president, was elected to the CEC.

A regular speaker at INTO Congress and at public meetings organised by the union, Bríd Bergin was nominated by the Minister to his Council of Education in 1950 (by then she had added a Higher Diploma in Education to her academic qualifications). In 1950 also, she was the only candidate sufficiently nominated for the INTO presidency and was declared elected. Her term as president included the signing of an agreement with the Minister establishing conciliation and arbitration machinery for teachers, and a function where she presented past president badges to a dozen prior holders of that office.

At Congress 1951 she called for two additional years of primary education, given that many pupils had to emigrate after schooling ended at age fourteen.

The Lady Teachers' Golfing Society, of which she was a member, made her a presentation to mark her presidential office. More than ten years after her term as president, she was (in a 1962 photograph in INTO's journal) captioned as Honorary Secretary of that Society.

Described by her predecessor president as 'a brilliant member of a brilliant family', Bríd Bergin died in 1976, her executors thanking sympathisers in a newspaper notice on 31 May of that year. An obituary in the *CEC Annual Report for 1976-1977* said that she would be 'remembered by the older members' as 'all through her teaching career a very energetic member of the INTO' and as being 'one of that vigorous group of ladies ....who, in the eventful days before and after 1946, fought hard on behalf of the welfare of lady teachers'.

Bríd Bergin on the picket line at the Department of Education in Marlborough Street, Dublin during the 1946 strike.

Margaret Skinnider (1892-1971)
President 1956-1957

Margaret Skinnider

Born in Scotland in 1892, Margaret Skinnider qualified as a teacher and began her career in Glasgow. Active in the Irish nationalist cause (her father was from Co Monaghan), she was wounded in the 1916 Rising in Dublin while serving with the Citizen Army. She participated in the subsequent War of Independence, and during the Civil War which followed she took the anti-Treaty side and was jailed for almost a year.

Afterwards she worked with the Workers' Union of Ireland before restarting her teaching career in 1927, serving until her retirement at the Sisters of Charity NS in King's Inns Street, Dublin. She lived from 1919 with her lifelong partner Nora O'Keeffe. In 1938 she was awarded a military service pension, thirteen years after making her application.

A member of the committee organising the Dublin-centred INTO pay strike of 1946, she led in pressing for salary negotiation machinery thereafter. By 1948 she was vice chair of the large Dublin City branch and the following year was elected to the CEC in a tightly-contested ballot. That same year she represented INTO on the Roe Committee on teacher remuneration. Elected unopposed to the CEC for several years following, she was often the only woman on INTO deputations and on the CEC, although her early term coincided with that of Brid Bergin as vice president and president. Active politically with Clann na Poblachta, she contested unsuccessfully for a seat on Dublin Corporation in 1950 and was on that party's national executive in 1953.

Margaret Skinnider was elected unopposed as INTO vice president in 1955, and to the presidency in 1956. As president, she represented INTO at the world teachers' conference in Manila, Philippines, writing extensively about her related journey in the INTO journal. She contested a Seanad seat on the Labour Panel in 1957 but was not elected. A dinner in her honour in October 1958 marked her nine years in INTO's central leadership.

Her union involvement was not over. She became chair of the Irish Congress of Trade Unions (ICTU) Women's Advisory Committee in 1959 and served on the ICTU executive in the early 1960s. In 1961, she told an INTO Congress debate that If teachers did not do something about conditions such as insanitary buildings and 'classes of 50, 60 or 70 pupils', they could not claim professional status. At Congress 1963 she was one of three previous or future woman presidents (Skinnider, Liston and Brennan) supporting a motion on equal pay for men and women; an amendment varying the proposal was passed by 184 votes to 122. Her guest address at INTO Congress 1966 marked the 50th anniversary of the Easter Rising.

Remarkably, she was listed as a Dublin City Congress delegate up to and including 1966.

Following her death in October 1971, she was buried in the republican plot at Glasnevin Cemetery.

Margaret Skinnider had her book *Doing My Bit for Ireland* published in 1917. Her activities are outlined in other publications including a biography by Mary McAuliffe (UCD Press, 2020), an article by Kirsty Lusk in *Saothar 41* (2016), Journal of the Irish Labour History Society, and an entry in the (online) *Dictionary of Irish Biography*, by Lawrence W White.

Margaret Skinnider leaving Dublin airport in 1956 for an international conference in the Philippines. She is seen off by, l to r, Liam O'Reilly (vice president), Dave Kelleher (general secretary) and Michael P Linehan (general treasurer).

Eileen Liston (1902-1984)
President 1965-1966

Eileen Liston

Born in July 1902 and growing up at Collierstown in east county Meath, Eileen Malin (later Liston) is recorded in the 1911 Census as 'Eily Josephine Malin'.

Following early teaching service in Co Meath at Dillonsbridge NS and Ashbourne, she worked for a year around 1939 on the same staff as Margaret Skinnider in King's Inns Street NS, Dublin. From 1940, as 'Mrs Eileen Liston', she taught at Christ the King NS, in Cabra.

Despite the example of previous woman activists, there were no women on the INTO executive committee, finance committee or Northern committee for 1961-'62. In that year, Eileen (sometimes 'Ellen') Liston was vice chair of Dublin City branch.

Unlike her predecessors, Eileen Liston did not have experience as a representative on the CEC prior to assuming the presidency. She gave notice of being a CEC district candidate in both 1962 and 1963 but it appears that all the branch nominations in each year went to the incumbent Matt Griffin.

In 1964, when serving also as chair of Dublin City branch, Liston was elected INTO vice president, her 63 per cent of the vote defeating a male candidate from Co Cork. As vice president she represented the union at a Needlework conference with the Department of Education. Returned unopposed as president in 1965, she was another notable proponent of equal pay. At this time the married men's pay scale was worth almost 20 per cent more than that of other teachers. As a branch delegate, Liston had taken on CEC members in argument on this issue at the 1963 Congress in a seminal debate on equality around a motion advocating equal pay for all national teachers.

Liston had a record of addressing INTO Congress on a range of issues including the 'archaic' Needlework programme (Congress 1959) and inadequate provision for school heating and cleaning (1963); after leaving national office she spoke about the issues affecting pensioners (1969).

The traditional presidential dinner in Liston's honour was held, at her request, in the Teachers' Club. Revised INTO Rules and structures were agreed from 1966 as a result of the work of a reorganisation committee which she chaired. While in the presidency, Eileen Liston was notified by general secretary Dave Kelleher of his proposed retirement in late 1966. Her handling of Congress that year was commended by Kelleher, particularly her chairing of the 'one very difficult debate'. This debate had culminated in a vote (by 200 to 121) to support Ministerial proposals on the 'integration of small schools'.

Her involvement with INTO continued after her presidency and following the splitting in two of the old Dublin City branch. She was on Dublin City North branch committee in 1971 and in the following year wrote movingly in the INTO journal about the sixth woman president Alice Brennan, as seen below.

Her father Patrick Malin had been principal of Skryne national school in county Meath. Eileen Liston's funeral took place at Skryne following her death on 3 June 1984.

Eileen Liston with Minister for Education George Colley in 1965, attending a Mass for Catholic teachers at the outset of the new school year.

Alice Brennan (1903-1972)
President 1971-1972

Alice Brennan

Alice Brennan was the only INTO president to die while in office. She was recalled movingly at her passing by her predecessor woman president Eileen Liston, her friend of forty-five years. Liston referred to Alice Brennan's convincing oratory delivered 'in her clear Dublin accent of which she was justly proud'. The great love of Alice Brennan's life, in tune with her Christian beliefs was, her friend said, 'her devotion to the underprivileged'.

While press reports at her death stated her year of birth as 1905, a cross-check of birth certificates, the 1911 census, and burial records indicates that she was the 'Alice Mary Dorothy' Brennan born in Dublin on 23 October 1903.

Alice Brennan qualified as a teacher from Carysfort College. She taught for almost all of her career (for more than thirty years) in Dublin's north inner city, at St Laurence O'Toole schools in Seville Place, initially in the senior girls' and later in the infants' school.

A district representative on the CEC from 1967 to 1970, she was the sole woman among the nineteen persons on the executive throughout those years, and on her election (unopposed) as vice president in 1970 and as president in 1971. She was a member of Dublin City North branch on election.

With a long record of addressing INTO Congress, several of her contributions were memorable. She spoke in 1963 and 1965, and as president in 1971, about deficits in school conditions and equipment. In 1968 she told of pupils in some city schools being 'underprivileged through bad housing conditions, neglect, and a variety of other factors'; she called for a lesser pupil-teacher ratio in such schools. She spoke at more than one Congress about supports – such as smaller classes and 'stackable' furniture - needed for 'modern methods' of teaching, as envisaged in the revised curriculum to be rolled out from 1971.

Alice Brennan was the third of the (past or future) woman presidents to speak on pay equality at the 1963 Congress. She criticised the CEC amendment – which would extend the married men's scale to widows (but not to other women or to single men). She asked why it was proposed that a widow who was childless would get the same pay as a married man when a single man would not.

On a motion concerning 'Remedial Teachers' in 1970 she suggested: 'Change the name of remedial teachers and give extra staff to the infants classes, and much of the difficulty will be overcome'. Unsurprisingly, she was INTO's nominee on the committee of the pioneering Van Leer preschool project in Dublin's inner city Rutland Street.

Some eight months into her term as INTO president, Alice Brennan died in a Raheny nursing home on 12 January 1972. Her death was certified as being due to a cerebral neoplasm. She was buried in Glasnevin Cemetery after which a reception for mourners took place in the Teachers' Club. Warm tributes in the INTO journal, led by Eileen Liston, included one from Tom Gilmore, a colleague on the INTO executive. He wrote that 'Alice Brennan could be relied upon for two qualities in particular, her courage and her plain speaking'.

Alice Brennan, the only woman on INTO's 1967-'68 executive committee (CEC) at the union's centenary. Of the nineteen persons in this photograph, fourteen (thirteen men and Alice) had held, then held or would hold the office of president. Two others – Quigley and Mackle – would later become general secretary and northern secretary, respectively. Seated: Alice Brennan, EG (Gerry) Quigley (northern secretary), Matt Griffin (general treasurer), Seán Brosnahan (general secretary), Jerry Allman (president), Alfred Faulkner (vice president), RS Holland (ex president), Tom Martin. Standing: Michael McKeown, Al Mackle, Seamus McArdle, Gerry Keane, Seán O'Brien, Seán Carew, Tom Gilmore, Seán O'Connor, Bernard Gillespie, Tom Warde, Brendan Scannell.

Fiona Poole
President 1978-1979

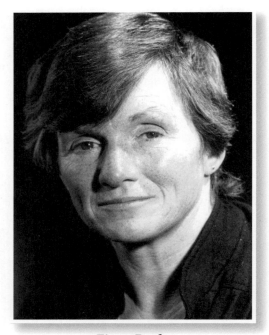

Fiona Poole

Fiona Poole (previously Hickey) was born in Cork city and raised in Kerry. She qualified as a teacher in 1954. Initially a student at the preparatory college at Coláiste Íde in Dingle, she then attended (1952-1954) in what she later described as the 'spartan and austere' atmosphere of Carysfort College of Education.

She taught (apart from a period spent in Germany and Singapore) in Dublin schools. Following her teaching in Singapore, she articulated the demands of those with service abroad as secretary of RETAG (the

Returned Emigrant Teachers' Action Group), setting out RETAG's policies in INTO's journal in 1974.

Active with Blackrock Teachers' (Education) Centre and as a lecturer on a range of topics, she had recognised expertise in the teaching of mathematics. She co-authored a series of school textbooks titled *Maths in Action* to coincide with promulgation of the revised primary school curriculum of 1971. At INTO Congress 1977, she criticised the situation where a male-dominated inspectorate had 'no training in Junior School work'.

Fiona Poole is unique among the woman presidents in not having contested the INTO vice presidency prior to becoming president, nor had she been a district representative on the CEC before her election. While chair of her INTO district she contested the presidency and set out her priorities through an election statement in the union journal *An Múinteoir Náisiúnta* in February 1978. Her opponent was the incumbent vice president, a member of Belturbet branch who had served for more than ten years on the CEC.

Teaching in Ballybrack and a member of South Co Dublin branch, Fiona Poole's presidential campaign stressed the need to improve members' participation and INTO's image, to tackle women teachers' grievances and to press for comprehensive professional development for teachers. During the contest, her activism with the Irish Family Planning Rights Association was highlighted in anonymous material, seeking to damage her electoral prospects.

Fiona Poole was elected as president, winning over 54 per cent of the votes to join an executive committee of nineteen where she was the only woman. As president she set out her view that provision for corporal punishment in schools should be ended, a policy later (1982) introduced by the Minister for Education.

Her presidency coincided with big changes in INTO's leadership, with the northern secretary elected as general secretary, and also taking up office in 1978 following a similarly hard-fought election.

Appointed to Dalkey (multidenominational) School Project in 1979, Fiona Poole later served as a CEC district representative from 1982 to 1988. In 1984, representing INTO at the Oireachtas Committee on Women's Rights, she criticised sexism in school textbooks where 'few of the women work outside the home … Equality ultimately must be seen to be practised'. A founding member of the Separated Teachers' Support Group in 1988, she remained active with that Group for many years, including after her retirement in 1996. In an article in the INTO journal of June 2003, she chronicled the formation and development of the Group.

Fiona Poole at a function held in her honour during her presidency, (l to r) general secretary Gerry Quigley, CEC colleague Tom Gilmore, Fiona Poole and Michael Moroney (general treasurer).

Róisín Carabine
President 1985-1986

Róisín Carabine

The first woman from Northern Ireland elected to the presidency, Belfast native Róisín Carabine qualified as a teacher having attended St Mary's College in that city from 1953 to 1956. At time of election as INTO president, she was vice principal at St Kevin's Girls' Primary School on the Falls Road where she had worked since qualification.

A member of INTO's Northern committee from 1975 (and chair of that committee in 1982), she won a contested election to become a district representative on the CEC where she served from 1979. She won election as vice president in 1984 in a ballot contested by two other candidates (both males) from Dublin and Waterford. Róisín Carabine secured 56 per cent of the vote. In her election statement, she began: 'I do not contest this election as a woman's candidate, a Northern candidate or a CEC candidate. I am contesting as an experienced, active INTO member '.

Her stated priority issues reflected some of the concerns of the day. Alongside the more standard demands for salary improvements and better resourcing of schools were items including greater professional autonomy for teachers, an equitable taxation system and the elimination of bias from appointment procedures.

Elected unopposed as president for 1985-1986, her term of office was particularly busy and public. The CEC which she chaired met on twenty-nine occasions from Congress 1985 to late February 1986. By comparison, it had met twenty-two times in a slightly longer period three years earlier. Her presidency was dominated by salary issues in both the Republic of Ireland and Northern Ireland. A pay dispute began in the North after deadlocked negotiations, while south of the border the three teacher unions, under the 'Teachers United' banner, campaigned to secure a pay award which had been made by an independent arbitrator.

As part of the 'Teachers United' campaign, President Carabine addressed some 20,000 striking teachers in Croke Park on 5 December 1985. Having previously accused the government of portraying teachers as 'parasites' and the administration of being 'more concerned about book-keeping than about justice', she told the Croke Park rally that the strike was organised 'in defence of our right to free collective bargaining'.

More than thirty years later she was a special guest at INTO Congress 2017 in Belfast where that dispute and her leadership in it were recalled.

In her presidential address to INTO Congress 1985, she announced that the teacher unions would charge the Irish government before the ILO (International Labour Organisation) with failing to honour ILO conventions regarding pay determination machinery. And in a context of ongoing violence in Northern Ireland, she advocated the teaching of respect for diverse value systems in order 'to promote attitudes of peace and tolerance'.

During her presidency, Roisín Carabine was appointed as principal of a new, large primary school, St Kieran's, in Poleglass, Belfast. In 2018, she was a guest at the Belfast launch of Niamh Puirséil's 150-year history of the INTO, *Kindling the Flame*, having offered insights into the union's work in Northern Ireland in an interview for that book.

Róisín Carabine addresses thousands of striking teachers in Croke Park, December 1985.

Sally Sheils
President 1995-1996

Sally Sheils

Dubliner Sally Sheils (previously Davis) was a graduate of the Church of Ireland College of Education and of Trinity College. She was a Dublin City South branch delegate to INTO Congress for several years when a teacher (and later principal teacher) in Sandford NS, Ranelagh. She spoke at Congress 1976 on class size issues and from early in her teaching career became involved in wider trade union organisation. As vice-president of Dublin Council of Trade Unions (DCTU) she addressed thousands of workers at the DCTU's May Day rally in 1982. In the same year she advocated at Congress that INTO's pay claim should be based on the average level of settlements in the private sector.

Sally Sheils' appointment as principal of the new North Dublin National School Project in 1984, at a time when she was serving both as her INTO branch chair and as DCTU vice president, resulted in her moving branch to Dublin City North. She remained prominent in the INTO, regularly speaking at Annual Congress, as in 1987 on sex education, and that same year was a strong voice in the union's opposition to Circular 20/1987 which increased class sizes. She told the press that discipline was 'definitely going to be a problem with larger classes'.

In 1989, she was elected as district representative to the CEC. During her five years in this role, and later in national leadership, she represented INTO on a range of bodies including the National Council for Curriculum and Assessment (NCCA) from 1995 to 1998, the Council of Teachers' Unions and the Education Advisory Committee of the Health and Safety Authority.

In 1994 she was elected as INTO's vice president and the following year as INTO president. At forty years of age she was one of the youngest presidents in INTO's history. In that office, she brought a particular focus on schools as part of their wider communities and on the lack of support services for children with special needs or who might be at risk. Described by journalist Nell McCafferty as an 'ardent, adept and committed trade unionist', soon after election she addressed a large march of striking INTO and ASTI members to highlight their retirement claim.

In July 1995 she represented INTO at Education International's world congress in Zimbabwe facilitating a group on the AIDS pandemic.

In her presidential address to Congress 1996, she demanded better resourcing of schools, saying: 'successive governments still cannot recognise that investing in primary education will save them substantial amounts of money later and all economists recognise that an educated population is essential to economic growth'.

For several years after her presidential term, and prior to her retirement in 2015, she contributed regularly as a delegate from the floor of INTO Congress. Asserting the rights of LGBTQ teachers, she was a strong opponent of the original section 37.1 of the Employment Equality Act (1998), later completing an M.Ed. thesis on this topic.

Sally Sheils speaks to a rally of teachers for better pension conditions, June 1995.

Joan Ward
President 2001-2002

Joan Ward

Dublin native Joan Ward (previously Hurley) qualified as a teacher from St Patrick's College in 1975. Her teaching career included service at Presentation convent NS Terenure where she had gone to school. She subsequently taught in Templeogue and later as deputy principal of Griffeen Valley ETNS, Lucan.

Elected to the INTO executive for district nine (south and west Dublin city) in 1988, she was the only woman on a CEC of twenty-one in the year of her election. During her two years as district representative, she contributed to Congress debates on educational broadcasting, teacher unemployment and as an advocate of teacher supply panels.

After standing down from the CEC, she represented INTO at the ICTU Women's Conference 1992, proposing a motion on family leave, and continued to serve on an INTO Steering Group overseeing a study of member participation. At Congress 1993 she criticised the Minister's failure to appoint a primary teacher to a Ministerial committee on bullying in schools, remarking: 'There would be uproar if doctors were excluded from a committee of experts established to investigate a medical matter'.

Joan Ward was elected unopposed as INTO vice president in 2000, the first woman qualified from St Patrick's College of Education to serve in that office. She was returned to the presidency the following year. As president, she described delays in setting up the planned National Educational Psychological Service as 'scandalous'.

Her presidential term coincided with the protests around access of children to Holy Cross Girls' Primary School in Belfast's Ardoyne and she visited that school in solidarity with members there. She called for education to be 'developed on an all-Ireland basis with teachers more directly involved in the process'. While president she also gave evidence for INTO to the Public Service Benchmarking Body in December 2001, a body which reported in July 2002.

In her presidential address to Congress 2002, Joan Ward contrasted the condition of a local primary school, within a few hundred metres of the Congress venue in Limerick, with the superb facilities of the University of Limerick. Recording that INTO was aware of over one hundred cases of substandard school buildings, she said that the school nearest the Congress location included 'a collection of second-hand, leaking prefabs long past their sell-by date'. She had earlier called on teachers and parents to make the physical condition of schools an issue in the 2002 general election.

Following her presidency, she served for periods on the INTO benefit funds and Congress standing orders committees. In 2004-2005, she successfully contested in the Dublin constituency the first election to the Teaching Council and was elected as first chair of the Council from 2005. Retiring from teaching in 2016, she has since served on a number of teacher disciplinary appeals panels and is chair of the Board of Management at an Educate Together national school.

Joan Ward launches INTO's booklet for parents – 'Your Child in the Primary School' – at Bishop Shanahan NS Dublin, with her sister Geraldine and niece Sinéad on Sinéad's first day at school.

Sheila Nunan
President 2005-2006

Sheila Nunan

A native of Newbridge, Co Kildare, a graduate of UCD and from St Patrick's College (1979), Sheila Nunan was the second of her family to become INTO president. Her Kerry grandfather Tom Nunan had served two terms in the presidency in the first half of the 20th century. Her teaching career included service in Tallaght and as a Visiting Teacher for Travellers. She featured in a profile of a busy branch secretary (of Tallaght branch) in the INTO journal of October 1991; she was later active in Craobh Chualann.

Sheila Nunan was principal of St Kieran's NS for Travellers in Bray, Co Wicklow when elected as a CEC district representative in 1995. She served from 1995 to 2004, representing the south Dublin and north Wicklow district. Appointed to represent INTO on the Council of the NCCA, she also served on the Schools Implementation Committee of the National Education Welfare Board.

Addressing Congress 1999 on tax evasion, she said: 'We have been staggered by the scale….and every evasion has a price tag for us as teachers'. She called for resources to support inclusion and told Congress 2003 that 'special education provision has been problem driven rather than vision led'.

Sheila Nunan was elected as vice president in 2004 and in this office she addressed the inaugural meeting of the union's Lesbian, Gay, Bisexual Teachers' (LGBT) Group. Becoming president in 2005, she later recalled as a proud moment leading INTO participants in the Irish Ferries workers' march against exploitation in December 2005.

In late 2005, she was elected as INTO deputy general secretary (taking office from 2006). In her presidential address to Congress 2006 she said that the country's prosperity had created the conditions for 'promoting a true equality of opportunity'. She included a call for curricular reform in Irish language teaching, especially in the junior and middle classes, saying: 'Let's do without textbooks, teach grammar through everyday usage and curb enthusiasm to correct every spelling mistake for that time'. She told delegates of her hopes that the newly-established Teaching Council would be an agent to promote high standards in areas including in-career development.

Sheila Nunan later became the first woman to hold the office (2010-2019) of INTO general secretary. She also served as president of the Irish Congress of Trade Unions from 2017 to 2019. As INTO general secretary, she led through successive pay negotiations and disputes during the fall-out from the economic collapse of 2008.

After retirement, she contested the European Parliament election in 2019 as a Labour Party candidate and served on a range of bodies including as chair of Comhar Linn INTO Credit Union, and on the boards of Maynooth University, the Institute of International and European Affairs (IEEA), and Early Childhood Ireland. In 2023, the Minister for Children appointed her to lead the process of negotiation with religious bodies which had a historical involvement in Mother and Baby and County Home institutions.

Sheila Nunan with general secretary John Carr at the INTO banner for a rally against the exploitation of Irish Ferries workers, 2006.

Angela Dunne
President 2007-2008

Angela Dunne

Shanagolden (Co Limerick) native Angela Dunne (previously Kennelly) was from a family where her five sisters also became teachers. She qualified into teaching from Mary Immaculate College in Limerick in 1966. In an era before free post-primary schooling, she recounted how her secondary education had been funded through the proceeds of her mother's chicken-keeping.

Angela taught from 1 July 1966 until her retirement in late 2009 at Ballinabranna NS, County Carlow. She additionally graduated from St Patrick's College with a B.Ed. degree in 1995. This was on the same day that her daughter Edel was also awarded a B.Ed. Angela Dunne was serving as vice principal of her school at the time of her election to the CEC in 1996.

An active member, and for several years secretary, of North Carlow INTO branch, she went on from 1996 to serve as district CEC representative for ten years. There she represented teachers in counties Carlow, Wexford, Kilkenny, Laois, and part of Wicklow. She was elected vice president in 2006, and as president the following year. The first woman who had qualified from Mary Immaculate College to become INTO president, she had a deep interest in special education, with a particular emphasis on catering for children with hearing impairment.

While a district representative on the CEC, she was appointed by the INTO to the Department of Education's Advisory Committee on the Education of the Deaf and Hard of Hearing, and also to the Review Group examining the Scrúdú Cáilíochta sa Ghaeilge process.

On becoming INTO president in 2007, Angela Dunne told the press that her priorities were decided by Annual Congress but she anticipated that they would include lowering class size, better funding for primary schools and highlighting the workload of teaching principals. The latter reflected her special interest in smaller schools, the 'heart of the community'. She said that she hoped to convince the Minister 'that all teaching principals should have one day off per week to do their administrative duties'.

Addressing Congress 2008 as president, she called for greater transparency in the school building process and questioned the state's capacity to make provision everywhere groups wished to open their own schools. Also on school buildings, she warned about heading back into 'crisis mode' in terms of available places and criticised a 'culture of secrecy' surrounding progress on building projects, demanding an open and transparent system be put in place. A strong campaigner for smaller class sizes, she stressed that the revised curriculum could not be implemented in classes of 30 to 37 pupils. Regarding the Irish language she demanded specific Irish research on language immersion strategies.

Following her presidential term, Angela Dunne was honoured at a civic reception hosted by Carlow County Council at which her work as a teacher in that county, and on behalf of her colleagues across the island, was recognised.

Angela Dunne meets Mary Golden during INTO Congress 2008 in Kilkenny to celebrate her 100th birthday: Mary's entire teaching career had been served in her native Co Kilkenny.

Máire Ní Chuinneagáin
President 2009-2010

Máire Ní Chuinneagáin

Packing INTO envelopes early as a child of teaching parents – her father Seán served on the INTO benefit funds committee – Corofin, Co Galway's Máire Ní Chuinneagáin initially attended Ballinderry NS where both of her parents (Úna and Seán) were teachers. After second-level education in Coláiste Mhuire, Tourmakeady, she qualified as a teacher in 1974 from

Mary Immaculate College, Limerick. On graduation, she was awarded the Carlisle and Blake premium as an outstanding student teacher. She taught in Scoil Fhursa, Gaillimh, a Modh Scoil lán-Ghaelach.

Máire was active from early in career in her Galway City branch and her district. She was elected to the INTO equality committee in 1987, becoming that committee's chair in 1990.

She was elected to the CEC, representing the Galway-Roscommon district, in 1997 and completed an M.Ed. degree in NUI Galway two years later. Active on several CEC committees, she was also a member of An Chomhairle um Oideachas Gaeltachta agus Gaelscolaíochta and a long-serving volunteer with Galway Mountain Rescue Team. She was a regular contributor at Annual Congress, an example being her proposal of a CEC motion in 2001 on children's access to the schools' psychological service.

Serving as vice president for 2008-2009 and chosen as INTO president in 2009, she was by then principal of Scoil Fhursa. She was acutely aware of the challenges of Ireland's financial crisis, telling Education Conference delegates that the country faced 'the most challenging times in living memory'. She spoke out against any plans for education cuts: 'We will look to protect the frontline education system for children. Education is the foundation of our recovery and the future'. She adopted the heartfelt mantra 'proud to be a public servant, proud to be a teacher' as a theme of her presidency.

As president, she continued to articulate a strong stand against cuts, alongside a commitment to quality education provision. She warned of 'the destruction and the undoing of all the things we have tried to build up for the education service over the last 40 years'. She deplored the position where ordinary workers were forced to help bail out 'financial joyriders' in the banking sector. Responding to an embargo on filling posts of responsibility in schools, she warned the government that they were 'not going to get this work done for nothing'. In 2009 she was elected to the executive council of the ICTU.

Her address to Annual Congress 2010 analysed the financial crisis and acknowledged anger at an agenda to drive down wages. She stressed the need to go beyond anger to a framework to overcome the crisis.

In recent years, following her retirement from teaching in 2015, Máire Ní Chuinneagáin has played an active role with Gambia Ireland Volunteers in Education, assisting in delivering a programme of professional development for teachers in that country. Active in the Retired Teachers' Association of Ireland, she is current (2024-2025) vice president of that body.

Máire Ní Chuinneagáin celebrates twenty-one years (1987-2008) of INTO's Equality Committee (of which she had been chair) with other chairs of that committee: l to r Patricia Shanahan, Máire Ní Chuinneagáin, Marjorie Murphy (first chair) and Eleanor O'Dwyer.

Noreen Flynn
President 2011-2012

Noreen Flynn

Qualifying from Carysfort College with the first B.Ed. class in 1977, Noreen Flynn initially taught for one year in her native Kinnegad, Co Westmeath. She subsequently worked in Dublin's south inner city, and would retire from her school there as principal teacher in 2020.

Having taught in New York during a career break, on return to Dublin in 1991 she became deeply involved with INTO, as a branch and district officer and tutor. Elected to the CEC in 1999 for south and west Dublin city, she represented the union on the statutory Educational Disadvantage Committee established under the 1998 Education Act.

She spoke on educational disadvantage at several Annual Congresses, highlighting the inadequacy of some schemes 'because they lacked the intensity necessary to make a real difference'. In 2005 she addressed this topic in an *InTouch* article and at the ICTU Conference, and in 2007 contributed to the publication *Beyond Educational Disadvantage* (Paul Downes and Ann Louise Gilligan, eds).

She completed a post graduate diploma in Educational Leadership in 2009 and two years later was appointed principal of Mater Dei Primary School, Basin Lane, Dublin.

Noreen Flynn was elected as INTO vice president in 2010 and to the presidency the following year. On election, she spoke of focussing on teacher employment as 2,000 new teaching graduates faced 'a slim possibility of finding work'. As INTO president she launched the union's good practice guidelines towards creating inclusive staff rooms. She said that teachers still witnessed or were confronted with homophobia. She sought positive action to 'help roll back discrimination until every staff room is an inclusive staff room'.

She called for a change in the law to correct an anomaly whereby under six-year-olds in school were not included under legislation on absenteeism.

Campaigning continued against cuts during the financial crisis. Noreen Flynn addressed large rallies in Dublin opposing threats to smaller schools, and to protest against cuts to teachers' allowances. She declared that 'Ireland cannot continue to load austerity on to the next generation'. She also spoke at an anti-austerity rally of thousands of teachers and parents in Letterkenny, Co Donegal, in March 2012. At Annual Congress 2012, as president she rejected the view that the country was 'in receivership' and promised that INTO would vigorously pursue a fairer future. She described a decision to remove incentives to teachers' further study as a false economy and damaging in the longer term.

Noreen Flynn's presidency included her participation with the INTO LGBT Group in the Dublin Pride March and a visit to Global Schoolroom projects in Assam, India. She also welcomed to the union's Education Conference her former lecturer, Nobel laureate Seamus Heaney.

In 2013, she facilitated the amalgamation of Mater Dei P.S. and Scoil San Séamus Christian Brothers' School (CBS). The transfer of the former CBS school to Educate Together was the first handover of a Catholic primary school to a different patron body.

Noreen Flynn with her former lecturer and Nobel laureate (1995) Seamus Heaney at INTO Education Conference 2011.

Anne Fay
President 2012-2013

Anne Fay

Making INTO history as the first woman immediately to succeed another woman as president, Anne Fay (previously Ryan) grew up in Cappawhite, Co Tipperary and in east Limerick. Her paternal grandparents had served as the teachers in a two-teacher school in Gortavalla in the parish of Doon, Co Limerick.

Following her secondary schooling in Doon, Anne graduated from NUI Maynooth. She received her primary teaching qualification from Mary Immaculate College, Limerick, one of a cohort in a 'fast track' teacher education scheme ('Wilson grads') aimed at tackling a teacher shortage. The scheme was amended to have the teacher education element precede teaching service, following INTO opposition to its original design.

In 1979, she began her professional career in Presentation NS, Fermoy, Co Cork where she taught for 23 years. From 2002 she was principal of St Joseph's NS, Fermoy. She retired from St Joseph's in 2014.

An active INTO member, she served as Fermoy branch secretary, as a district trade union training tutor, and from 1997 on INTO's education committee where she presented on a range of topics at Education Conferences.

She was elected as CEC district representative for Cork city north, and north and east county Cork, in 2004. While on the CEC she was deeply involved in the development of, and practice in, the area of early childhood education. She represented INTO on the Early Childhood Committee of the NCCA and the Education Committee of Inclusion Ireland. She proposed a Congress motion on early childhood education in 2006, and regularly represented INTO, and presented at, conferences of the European Early Childhood Education Research Association.

Anne Fay became vice president of INTO in 2011 and was elected as president the following year. Another president who served during the economic recession – aptly describing her time on the CEC as 'the best of times followed by the worst of times' - she warned against attempts to close smaller schools. On pay inequalities, she stressed: 'We're working seriously hard to soften the financial blow being caused to new teachers working alongside people who are being paid much more than them'.

At INTO Congress 2013 Anne Fay condemned 'selective leaks' from a value-for-money report on smaller schools. Chairing an INTO task force on the topic, she warned that over a thousand schools feared for their existence.

An INTO representative on a range of educational bodies, she particularly advocated reduction in numbers in junior classes where play was used educationally, saying that: 'Using play and focussing on interaction to promote learning … is impossible in classes with over 30 infants'.

Following her retirement, she worked with 'INTO Learning', overseeing its professional development programme of summer 2015. She is active with the CPSMA (Catholic Primary School Management Association). She was elected to its board of directors in 2018, led in training members of boards of management, and became CPSMA chairperson in 2021. She chairs two primary school boards in the Fermoy area.

Anne Fay addresses teachers at a rally for pay equality, 2012, following pay cuts imposed on new entrant teachers from 2011.

Emma Dineen
President 2015-2016

Emma Dineen

Originally from Inniscarra, Co Cork, Emma Dineen (née Kelly) attended Dripsey primary school and St Aloysius Girls' secondary school in Cork city. She qualified as a teacher from the St Patrick's College postgraduate course in 1978. She had previously graduated (in history and Irish) from UCC in 1977, returning there to complete an M.Ed. degree in 1998.

With employment uncertain after qualification, she spent some two years doing substitute work before securing a permanent position at Cloghroe NS. A large school on the outskirts of Cork city, Cloghroe is where she spent the remainder of her teaching career, with a period of secondment to the Primary Curriculum Support Programme (PSCP) as a tutor.

She was active in INTO's Coachford branch, becoming her branch, and later her district, chairperson. Elected in 2000 to the education committee, she was a regular presenter at INTO Education Conferences. In 2001, speaking on the conference theme of change in education, she stressed that securing 'teacher professional belief must surely be one of the starting points in any successful change programme'.

Emma Dineen was elected to the CEC in 2005, representing members in the south side of Cork city, and in the county west to Castletownbere. Committed to trade union training, she served for many years as a staff representative tutor. She worked on NCCA committees dealing with PE and with Primary Education. In 2007 she advocated for a nationwide system of induction and mentoring for young teachers.

She was appointed principal of Cloghroe NS in 2012, prior to her election as INTO president in 2015. As some recession-era pay cuts were ameliorated through campaigning and negotiations, she was the first chair of INTO's project team on pay equality which ultimately reported to Congress 2017. She warned of the implications of young teachers emigrating due to pay cuts.

Early in her presidency she called on the Department to 'wake up to the crisis in school leadership'. She told the Education Conference that what constituted essential school learning should always be contested because behind this is a much-needed debate about what is of most worth in education. One of her presidential duties was representing the INTO at the Education International conference in Ottawa.

With her term including the early months of 2016, Emma Dineen reflected in the national press on schooling at the time of the 1916 Rising, referencing differences in curricula, teacher education and inspection. An advocate for education reform and development, she represented INTO on the council of the NCCA.

Emma Dineen has a long history of playing and coaching camogie and hurling and of involvement in schools' games through the Sciath na Scol competitions in Cork. She participated in the compilation of the history of this competition. Retiring from teaching in March 2021, she is currently a tutor with MIC Limerick, supporting student teachers on school placement.

Emma Dineen presents an honorary INTO president's medal to Martina Johnson, long-serving chair of the Benefit Funds Committee, at INTO Congress 2016.

Rosena Jordan
President 2016-2017

Rosena Jordan

From Castlebar, Co Mayo, Rosena Jordan qualified as a teacher from Carysfort College in 1982, a time of recession and significant teacher unemployment. She taught in Co Cavan, at Carrickaleck NS Kingscourt from 1983, and from 2004 at Virginia. She was active in her local INTO branches (Carrickmacross and Cavan East) and in her district from the 1980s.

She was elected to the INTO education committee in 2003 and served there for five years. Among her presentations at INTO Education Conference was one in 2005 which examined early childhood care and education provision. She represented INTO on NCCA committees on Language and on Early Childhood Education.

In 2008, Rosena Jordan was elected, following a contested bye-election, as district CEC representative for counties Louth, Cavan, and Monaghan. This contest arose from the untimely death of her CEC predecessor Peter McGrane.

She served as district representative for seven years prior to her election as vice president in 2015 and as president the following year. In those offices, she prioritised restoration of pay equality for post-2010 entrants to teaching. Addressing a large rally in October 2016, she said that progress had been made but the fight for pay equality would go on. She chaired the INTO project team on pay equality which reported to INTO Congress 2017, and addressed teachers and media at a pay rally at Queen's University Belfast in March 2017.

Her presidency coincided with centenary commemorations of the 1916 Rising. She attended and spoke at INTO-linked events including the naming of the Margaret Skinnider roundabout in Monaghan town and a ceremony recalling another 1916 combatant, Thomas Ashe, at the school where he had taught, Corduff NS in north Co Dublin. Her attendance at Workers' Memorial Day events and her membership of ICTU's Health and Safety Committee, where she was vice-chair from 2017 to 2021, reflected her broader trade union commitment.

Rosena Jordan's presidential address to INTO Congress 2017 summarised the challenges for the union, across members' priority areas, as the need to 'overturn the unfairness of the present and to work together for a fairer future'. At the close of her speech, she referenced issues of global human rights, advocating that the United Nations (UN) sustainable goal for education be a 'cornerstone' of trade union work.

A lover of the arts and of sport, she has performed in choirs and with Cavan drama groups. In her student years she had won provincial titles in athletics, and in national soccer competitions with Carysfort College. She was in 2020 the first elected female officer on the Cavan Gaelic Athletic Association (GAA) County Board and was Ulster Scór secretary with the GAA.

In 2020, she was elected to the Teaching Council, in the Connacht-Ulster constituency, for the 2020-2024 term. She retired from teaching in November 2020 and is currently an officer with Cavan Cumann na mBunscol and a member of ICTU's Health and Safety committee.

Rosena Jordan keeps up the fight against new entrant pay cuts, speaking at an INTO rally at Leinster House, October 2016.

Mary Magner
President 2020-2021

Mary Magner

Like Rosena Jordan, Mary Magner (also known as Ita Ahern) graduated in 1982 at a time of high unemployment. Having qualified from St Patrick's College, she began her teaching career in inner city Dublin. A native of Castletownroche Co Cork, she then taught in a number of Cork schools before settling at St Patrick's BNS, Mallow, from 1995. Following a career break which began in 1988 and where she indulged her passion for travel, she served as an officer of Mallow branch and as secretary of her INTO district.

While teaching, she graduated with a Masters in ICT in Education from Mary Immaculate College, Limerick, and further studied a postgraduate diploma in Special Education Needs in University College Cork.

She served as both an acting teaching principal and administrative principal in Mallow, later moving to Scoil Chroí Íosa in Blarney where she served as principal from 2014.

Elected to the CEC in 2011, she represented north Cork City and north and east county Cork. Her terms as vice president (2019-2020) and as president (2020-2021) were marked by the effects of the COVID19 pandemic which heralded restrictions on movement and in other areas (including school closures) from Spring of 2020. An *InTouch* headline in May 2020 declared that: 'Despite Congress being postponed the work must go on'. Accordingly, Mary Magner chaired meetings of the CEC and of other committees remotely, engaged with the Department and other education organisations similarly, and met numerous members while sitting at her screen.

She commended teachers, in a context of school closures and online engagement, for 'upskilling and providing new learning platforms for pupils, often going beyond the call of duty'. She wrote in *InTouch* reflecting on topics such as school leadership in the health crisis, and referred to some positive environmental outcomes worldwide arising out of the pandemic. The climate change issue is one which she has worked on with the charity Self Help Africa. She addressed online Youth Conferences of INTO members on either side of the island's border in January and March 2021, respectively. In the public health context, she pushed hard for and helped secure additional supports for schools during the pandemic, giving evidence at the Special Oireachtas Committee on the COVID19 Response.

Mary Magner's presidential Congress in 2021 was a hybrid event. She chaired from, and some INTO personnel attended at, a venue in Co Kildare while delegates generally contributed to the Congress via video link. Her main address reflected on 'an unprecedented presidential year' which, alongside the perennial resource issues, had highlighted the IT disparity between schools and the lack of supports such as counsellors for the most vulnerable pupils. She applauded the strength and resilience of teachers in the face of the pandemic-related challenges.

Mary Magner retired from her principal position in 2023 and continues to represent INTO on the Teaching Council, chairing that body's Finance Committee.

Mary Magner talks with children at a Dublin school in a typically 'socially distanced' outdoor engagement during the COVID-19 pandemic in 2020.

Dorothy McGinley
President 2023-2024

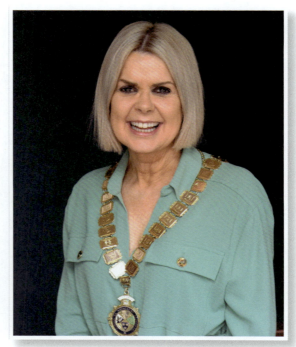

Dorothy McGinley

Dorothy McGinley grew up in the same village (Annagry, Co Donegal) as current INTO general secretary John Boyle, and graduated as a teacher from St Patrick's College, Dublin (since 2016 part of Dublin City University) in 1986. She taught for one year in Donegal before spending nine years teaching in various international school systems including the USA, Scotland, India, and Ethiopia. She subsequently returned to teach in Northern Ireland, working for three consecutive summers with Global Schoolroom teacher education projects in India and Africa.

Dorothy was for a number of years branch secretary/treasurer of her Strabane branch. She served on the INTO education committee for one year prior to her election to the CEC in 2012. Also a member of INTO's Northern committee from 2012, she chaired that committee in 2017-2018. On the day of a major public service anti-austerity strike in Northern Ireland in March 2015, she addressed a crowd of several thousand at Guildhall Square, Derry.

In 2017 she travelled to the Palestinian West Bank as part of a *Trade Union Friends of Palestine* delegation. She was deeply affected by the suffering of and restrictions imposed on Palestinian people and educators; she subsequently spoke about this on a number of occasions and wrote about it in January 2018's *InTouch* magazine.

From 2012 until her election as INTO vice president in 2022, she represented her INTO district (comprising counties Derry, Tyrone, Fermanagh, Armagh, and South Down) on the CEC. At her election to the presidency, she worked as a teacher at Sion Mills Primary School in Co Tyrone. She has written in the INTO's journal about her school's children and their activism on social issues; their climate change work (2019) and their challenging of Stormont's Infrastructure Minister on his visit to their school (2023).

Soon after being elected as president in April 2023, Dorothy McGinley accompanied members on the picket line at Sacred Heart College, Omagh, as part of a Northern Ireland-wide teachers' strike on pay issues. This activity rhymed with her stated mantra as president that society should 'value education, value our profession'. In March 2024 she was a delegate at the *68th Session on the Status of Women* at the UN headquarters in New York which highlighted the exclusion from education of tens of millions of girls worldwide.

At Congress 2024 in Derry, she summarised the most positive aspects of her presidential year as witnessing: 'children flourishing, being empowered by outstanding educators and enjoying their own agency.' She emphasised, however, that without the necessary supports, the commitment of teachers 'comes at a human cost to our members,' and that teacher burnout is an issue of concern. She concluded with a call for a forum on all-Ireland education.

Following her term as president, Dorothy McGinley returned to her teaching position in Sion Mills Primary School. From September 2024 this has become an integrated school under the Council for Integrated Education in Northern Ireland.

Dorothy McGinley celebrates 100 years of the Teachers' Club (2023) with (l to r) Club chief executive Tadhg Mac Pháidín, Dorothy McGinley, Club president Anita Hogan and INTO general secretary John Boyle.

Carmel Browne
President 2024-2025

Carmel Browne

A native of Cloonfad, Rooskey, Co Roscommon, Carmel Browne's sporting background, prior to becoming a teacher and since then, is extensive. It has included winning an All-Ireland senior football medal with Roscommon in 1978 and serving for several years as secretary of Longford Town Football Club.

Carmel began her teaching career and joined the INTO in 1980. During that career she taught in London for several years. Later, as a teacher in Longford, she was elected to the INTO equality committee.

She and other members of the equality committee engaged in interview-based research concerning teachers' mental health, presenting findings to the Equality Conference in 2013. She wrote an article about this mental health research in *InTouch* the following year. In 2014 also she spoke to an INTO motion on this topic at the ICTU Women's Conference.

In 2015, she presented a workshop on Physical Activity at INTO's Education Conference. This presentation drew on research conducted for her Masters in Education degree, which had been awarded in 2011.

When INTO organised a major conference on Special Education in 2015, she was a member of the working group which planned the event. In the recent past, she was an expert participant on the panel dealing with issues raised by delegates at an INTO Symposium on Special Education in February 2024.

Carmel Browne was chair of the union's equality committee when elected to the CEC in 2015. The CEC district which she represented is geographically extensive and the INTO's largest in membership terms, encompassing counties Longford, Westmeath, Offaly, Kildare, and Meath. On election to the executive she called for solidarity among INTO members to recover and protect pay and conditions. In this context, she was an active participant on INTO's project team on pay equality (2015-2017) and chaired INTO's recent task force on pay and pensions (2023-2024).

When elected as vice president in 2023, and to the presidency in 2024, she was serving as deputy principal of Melview NS in Longford town where she has taught since 1998. Her inaugural address as incoming president referred to her family and how, as the youngest of eight, she and her siblings were encouraged to strive to be their 'true selves', to remain grounded, dream big, respect others, and embrace challenge. She committed to 'advocate for equality, inclusion, and human rights, with as a priority to engage with stakeholders to support members to better the lives of the most vulnerable pupils'.

Carmel Browne is an INTO representative on the Council of the NCCA (2022-2026). An advocate for inclusive education, she believes that new innovative curriculum specifications will help enhance pupils' and teachers' school lives in coming years. As this publication is being finalised (January 2025), there are some months until she hands over the president's chain of office at the end of Easter Congress 2025, a Congress which she will chair and where she will deliver the presidential address.

Carmel Browne with President of Ireland Michael D Higgins who celebrated the contribution of trade unions to Irish society at Áras an Uachtaráin, 2024.

Anne Horan
President-elect 2025-2026

Anne Horan

Anne Horan (previously Burke) is a native of west Cork who now lives in Co Limerick. Having attended her local primary school in Ballineen, her post-primary education was at Presentation Convent in Bandon. She qualified as a teacher from Mary Immaculate College in Limerick, and joined the INTO, in 1980.

Anne began her teaching career with six years at Dunmanus NS, a one-teacher school on the Mizen Peninsula where she was a member of INTO's

Schull branch. A similar period was spent as a substitute and temporary teacher in the recessionary years of the 1980s into the early 1990s, before being appointed to a post in St Fergus NS, Glin, Co Limerick. Anne is currently principal of the three-teacher Carrickerry NS in west Limerick, and is a member of Glin INTO branch.

Active in the union over several years, Anne Horan has served as a staff representative and as a staff representative tutor. She also served with the INTO as a primary science tutor. She has undertaken professional development on a regular basis, including as a current PhD student at Mary Immaculate college. In addition, she is a cardiac first responder, and a cardiac first responder community instructor, with the Irish Red Cross. Her vital skills in this regard were decisive following a public incident of cardiac arrest, as outlined in INTO's journal *InTouch* (December 2016).

In 2012, Anne Horan was elected to the union's benefit funds committee, representing the Munster division covering counties Cork, Kerry, and Limerick. She was elected as INTO district representative for counties Limerick and Kerry on the CEC in 2015 and served in that role for nine years.

Her election as vice president in 2024 made history as, for the first time in INTO's 156 years, the union's president, vice president and immediate ex-president (for 2024-2025) are all women. Anne Horan is scheduled to take up office as INTO's 21st woman president – and the first female president from her district – at Easter Annual Congress 2025.

Three INTO Woman Presidents, 2023-2026

Three successive women presidents, for the first time since INTO was founded in 1868, at a function to honour Carmel Browne in the office, October 2024:
l to r Dorothy McGinley (president 2023-2024), Carmel Browne (2024-2025),
and Anne Horan (elected for 2025-2026).

Conclusion

Soon after her election to the CEC and four years before becoming INTO's first woman president, Catherine Mahon addressed 'lady teachers' in Cork. The address was reported under the headline 'Ladies and the Organisation' (*Irish School Weekly*, 18 January 1908, p.684). She challenged her audience by saying: 'I do not see why we should not take exactly the same interest in the Organisation as the men teachers'.

Reserved Seats Attract Candidates

Powerful advocate for women though Mahon was, the lower level of female participation was hardly due to a lack of interest, or to this factor alone. One must look at many other aspects, including the roles presumed appropriate to women, to explain why the INTO executive committee had been an all-male preserve until 1907.

The difference made in 1907 was the creation of two reserved seats for women. These brought Belfast's Elizabeth Larmour and Birr's Catherine Mahon into the leadership. The existence of these places for some ten years demonstrated no lack of interest among women in serving on the CEC. In 1914, for example, ten candidates received nominations for the principal teachers' reserved seat while eight women were nominated for the analogous assistant teachers' position.

It is probable that Catherine Mahon's remarks in Cork were intended to challenge and motivate listeners rather than to posit lack of interest as a major reason for lesser female representation in the union's structures.

Subordinate Place

TJ O'Connell recalled that until the 1890s only men principals were eligible to contest CEC positions. Under O'Connell's lengthy tenure as general secretary (1916-1948), however, the participation of women in leadership positions scarcely improved. That was especially so after the removal from 1918 of reserved seats and the introduction of a system whereby four geographical districts each returned a principal and an assistant teacher to the CEC.

O'Connell's view was that: 'As they constituted 60 per cent of the membership, it was thought that women would be strongly represented on any future Executive' (O'Connell 1968, p.274). He observed that: 'In the thirty years during which this (four district) system operated only one woman principal – Miss K Tierney of Mallow – was elected to the Executive as district representative, though a number of women were elected during that period as assistants' representatives' (O'Connell 1968, p.14).

In the years between 1919 and 1947 no more than seven women, in total, served on the CEC (see Appendix 3, section B, for a listing of the five who did not become president). This total of seven includes Kathleen Clarke who was an assistant teachers' district representative for several years before becoming president, and Bríd Bergin who was a principals' representative at the end of this period. The women elected to the CEC in these years, and who did not become president, tended to serve on the executive briefly.

The 1930s were especially challenging times for women teachers with the introduction of a ban on the continuation in service of married women and of those over 60 years of age. The compulsory retirement regulation remained in place until 1948, the marriage bar until 1958. The existence and longevity of these provisions, directed only at women, were powerful indications of the state's view of the subordinate place of female teachers and of women generally.

Uneven Progress

Since 1947 one representative per district, irrespective of teaching role, is elected to the INTO executive.

The effects of the lengthy salary strike of 1946 on the INTO were profound and (for a time at least) brought women, and a new cohort of men, into greater prominence in the union. Two of the dispute's main protagonists – Seán Brosnahan and Matt Griffin – went on to lead the INTO into the late 1970s as general secretary and deputy general secretary/general treasurer, respectively.

The next four woman presidents after Kathleen Clarke were strikers from 1946. They served within a period of a little over twenty years (1950 – 1972). By contrast, the twenty-two years following (1972 to 1994) saw just two women elected as president.

It was only from the 1990s that the number of females in the central leadership of the INTO started to increase. When Joan Ward was elected as a district representative to the CEC in 1988, she was the only woman on an executive of twenty-one (fifteen district representatives and six office-holders). This was the last occasion in which this situation pertained. By 1996, there were four women on the executive, by 1999 there were six as district representatives.

Building Momentum

Similarly, the representation of women among INTO presidents increased from the start of the 21st century. Eleven of the twenty INTO women presidents to date have been elected since the year 2000.

While progress in the number of women in leadership may be attributed in part to societal change, there were internal union factors behind this also. In 1980, Catherine Byrne was appointed as the union's first woman official since Mairéad Ashe had left in 1927. Her appointment 'would prove crucial to the INTO's efforts to modernise its policies on gender' (Puirséil 2017, p 162). She was designated as equality officer in 1982 and an INTO equality committee was created in 1987.

Participation studies and the regular publication of gender-segregated statistics on areas such as promotion in teaching and office-holding in the INTO reflected a move to tackle earlier disparities. Further women were appointed as officials of the union at head office. Anne McElduff was the first of these, going on to become an assistant general secretary in 2002, a position to which a number of women have been appointed subsequently.

Milestone and Trajectory

While debates continue about participation in the union and around gender aspects of this, progress can be reported. This publication marks one milestone, with a focus on the INTO presidency as the 20th woman in that office is about to be succeeded by the 21st.

This is a milestone but twenty (soon to be twenty-one) women in the presidency is a low number in the context of the membership's gender profile. Each of the presidents highlighted here may be considered to be, literally, exceptional.

Progression towards more balanced gender representation in the INTO has not been linear but the trajectory in this direction, including among presidents, now appears more consistent and sustained.

At INTO Annual Congress, the president's role includes delivering a keynote address and chairing the gathering, as illustrated in these photographs.

Joan Ward chairs at Congress 2002, alongside general secretary Joe O'Toole at his final INTO Congress before retirement.

Angela Dunne, delivering her presidential address at INTO Congress 2008.

Emma Dineen chairs Congress 2016, alongside general secretary Sheila Nunan and broadcaster Joe Duffy who gave a guest address on the theme of children and the 1916 Rising.

Mary Magner delivers her presidential address to camera at INTO Congress 2021 where the COVID-19 pandemic prevented an assembly of delegates at one venue.

APPENDICES

Appendix 1

INTO Presidents 1868 – 2025 (woman presidents in bold type)

1868 – 1873: Vere Foster

1873 - 1875: John Boal

1875 - 1877: John Traynor

1877 - 1882: John Ferguson

1882: William Cullen

1883 - 1889: John Nealon

1889 - 1892: Philip Ward

1892 - 1897: D.A. Simmons

1897: Dr. Terence Clarke

1898: Robert Brown

1899 - 1904: James Hegarty

1904: John Nealon

1905: J. J. Hazlett

1906: Denis C Maher

1907: Patrick Gamble

1908: David Elliott

1909: James McGowan

1910: Eamonn Mansfield

1911: George O'Callaghan

1912 - 1914: Catherine M. Mahon

1914 - 1916: George O'Callaghan

1916: George Ramsay

1917: James Cunningham

1918: Robert Judge

1919: Tom Nunan

1920: Denis C. Maher

1921: John Harbison

1922: Cormac Breathnach

1923: Dennis Meehan

1924: John Mc Neelis

1925: Cornelius P. Murphy

1926: Thomas Frisby

1927: Hugh O'Donnell

1928: P.J. Quinn

1929: Eugene Caraher

1930: William P. Ward

1931: Robert Neilly

1932: Michael Kearney

1933: Cormac Breathnach T.D.

1934: Jeremiah Hurley T.D.

1935: Liam McSweeney

1936: DF (Frank) Courell

1937: Seán F. O'Grady

1938: Tom Nunan

1939: Martin Leyden

1940: H. A. Macaulay

1941: James P. Griffith

1942: Michael Coleman

1943: Hugh O'Connor

1944: Thomas Frisby

1945: Kathleen M. Clarke

1946: Dave Kelleher

1947: Seán Brosnahan

1948: Liam Forde

1949: Joseph Mansfield

1950: Bríd Bergin

1951: Ignatius H McEnaney

1952: Paddy Gormley

1953: Harry J. McManus

1954: Matt Griffin

1955: Capt. H. F. McCune-Reid

1956: Margaret Skinnider

1957: Liam O'Reilly

1958: Gerald Hurley

1959: William Keane

1960: Seán McGlinchey

1961: P. J. Looney

1962: Patrick O'Riordan

1963: Dónal Ó Scanaill

1964: Pat Carney

1965: Eileen Liston

1966: R. S. Holland

1967: Jerry Allman

1968: Alfred J. Faulkner

1969: Tom Martin

1970: Tommy Warde

1971: Alice Brennan

1972: Seán O'Connor

1973: Seán O'Brien

1974: Seán Carew

1975: Denis Eustace

1976: Bernard Gillespie

1977: Brendan Scannell

1978: Fiona Poole

1979: Gerry Keane

1980: Michael McSweeney

1981: Frank Cunningham

1982: Tom Waldron

1983: Morgan O'Connell

1984: John Joe Connelly

1985: Roísín Carabine

1986: Séamus Puirséil

1987: Tom Honan

1988: Michael Drew

1989: Tom Gilmore

1990: John White

1991: Jimmy Collins

1992: Brendan Gilmore

1993: Eddie Bruton

1994: Michael McGarry

1995: Sally Sheils

1996: Liam McCloskey

1997: Tony Bates

1998: Brian Hynes

1999: Des Rainey

2000: Dónal Ó Loingsigh

2001: Joan Ward

2002: Gerry Malone

2003: Seán Rowley

2004: Austin Corcoran

2005: Sheila Nunan

2006: Denis Bohane

2007: Angela Dunne

2008: Declan Kelleher

2009: Máire Ní Chuinneagáin

2010: Jim Higgins

2011: Noreen Flynn

2012: Anne Fay

2013: Brendan O'Sullivan

2014: Seán McMahon

2015: Emma Dineen

2016: Rosena Jordan

2017: John Boyle

2018: Joe Killeen

2019: Feargal Brougham

2020: Mary Magner

2021: Joe McKeown

2022: John Driscoll

2023: Dorothy McGinley

2024: Carmel Browne

2025: Anne Horan

Appendix 2

INTO's central executive committee (CEC) 2024-2025

The current CEC is listed to indicate that the gender balance has much changed since the years up to the 1990s when this body generally was an all-male one, or included a solitary woman.

Office Holders:

President - Carmel Browne

Vice President - Anne Horan

Ex President - Dorothy McGinley

General Secretary - John Boyle

Deputy General Secretary & General Treasurer - Deirdre O'Connor

Northern Secretary - Mark McTaggart

District Representatives:

1. Seamus Hanna
2. Annemarie Conway
3. Áine McGinley
4. Máire C English
5. Adrian Kelly
6. Gerard Murray
7. Peter O'Toole
8. Gerry Brown
9. Orlaith Ní Fhoghlú
10. Deirdre Fleming
11. Brendan Horan
12. Edel Polly
13. Tracie Tobin
14. Joanne Marie Doyle
15. Máire Lineen
16. Siobhán Buckley

Appendix 3

Women CEC representatives (1907-2025) who have not served as president (and men in the same category since 1975)

Names and titles are given as in INTO records; where an INTO district/area comprises more than one county, only the town/city and/or county where the executive committee member was teaching at time of service is listed. Current CEC representatives are not included as they are already listed at <u>Appendix 2</u>.

There had not been a woman on the INTO executive prior to 1907.

The designation 'Assistant' or 'Assistant Teacher' was applied to a qualified teacher who was not the Principal Teacher of a school. Into the early 20th century, most teachers were principals: the *Commissioners for National Education Report for 1908-1909* recorded the teaching force as including 8,026 principals and 4,705 assistants.

Women CEC Representatives

A. 1907-1918: Two reserved executive committee positions for females (one Principal and one Assistant Teacher):

➤ Elizabeth E Larmour (Belfast), Assistants' Representative

➤ Miss E MacNeill (Belfast), Principals' Representative

➤ Mrs Mary A Byrne (Milford St School, Belfast), Principals' Representative

➤ Miss Maisie Mangan (Killarney, Co Kerry), Assistants' Representative

➤ Miss LM (Margaret) Doyle MA (Dublin), Assistants' Representative

B. 1919-1947: Reserved seats abolished – CEC comprises two representatives (one Principal, one Assistant) from each of four 'North, South, East and West' divisions/provinces:

➤ Miss Katie Tierney (Buttevant, Mallow, Co Cork), Principal

- ➢ Mrs Mary E Stack (Claremorris, Co Mayo), Assistant
- ➢ Miss N O'Driscoll (Limerick), Assistant
- ➢ Miss Norah Higgins (Foxford, Co Mayo), Assistant/Mrs N McGovern (Foxford, Co Mayo), Assistant *[Norah Higgins, schoolteacher, married Vincent P McGovern in Castlebar on 2 September 1946: it is most probable that N Higgins and N McGovern are the same person. The ban on women continuing as teachers after marriage affected those entering teaching from October 1934; presumably Ms Higgins/ McGovern was in service before that date].*
- ➢ Miss Margaret Ambrose (Cork), Assistant

C. 1948-Present: Election of one representative per geographical district (initially ten districts, from 1968 thirteen districts, from 1983 fifteen districts, from 1994 sixteen districts):

- ➢ Mrs B Lally BA (District 2, Co Armagh)
- ➢ Marjorie Murphy (District 15, Dublin)
- ➢ Áine O'Neill (District 15, Dublin)
- ➢ Mary Lally (District 15, Dublin)
- ➢ Helen O'Gorman (District 7, Co Longford)
- ➢ Mary Cahillane (District 1, Belfast)
- ➢ Mary McIntyre (District 3, Co Donegal)
- ➢ Claire Byrne (District 10, Co Wexford)
- ➢ Mary O'Flaherty (District 9, Dublin)
- ➢ Margaret Bernard (District 13, Co Limerick)
- ➢ Catherine Flanagan (District 5, Co Monaghan)
- ➢ Carmel Hume (District 9, Dublin)

Men CEC Representatives

This listing dates from 1975 to date, broadly sequentially. To have gone back to the foundation of the INTO would entail very substantial research beyond the main purpose of this publication and the resulting list would contain an enormous number of names.

- ➢ John Blake (North Dublin)
- ➢ Al Mackle (Co Armagh)
- ➢ Seamus McArdle (Co Cavan)
- ➢ Joe O'Toole (North Dublin)
- ➢ Michael McKeown (Belfast)
- ➢ S. O'Donnell (Co Donegal)
- ➢ Tim Galvin (Co Wexford)
- ➢ John Carr (North Dublin)
- ➢ Danny McAllister (Belfast)
- ➢ Noel Ward (South Dublin)
- ➢ Tom O'Sullivan (Limerick city)
- ➢ PJ McEvoy (Co Down)
- ➢ Paddy O'Neill (Cork city)
- ➢ Maurice Kearney (Co Meath)
- ➢ Liam McGowan (Co Donegal)
- ➢ Justin McCarthy (Cork city)
- ➢ Tony Lappin (Co Derry)
- ➢ Gerry Ruddy (Belfast)
- ➢ John McGroarty (Co Donegal)
- ➢ Peter McGrane (Co Cavan)
- ➢ Seamus Long (Limerick city)
- ➢ Donal O'Donoghue (North Dublin)
- ➢ Gerry McGeehan (Co Donegal)
- ➢ Pat Stenson (Co Sligo)
- ➢ Charlie Glen (Derry city)
- ➢ Bryan O'Reilly (Co Kildare)
- ➢ Michael Weed (Co Donegal)

- Pat Crowe (North Dublin/North Kildare)
- Shane Loftus (North Dublin)
- Vincent Duffy (Co Mayo)
- Tommy Greally (Co Galway)
- Gregor Kerr (North Dublin)

List of Main Sources

While certain other sources (e.g. relevant articles, State records, and certain entries in the *Dictionary of Irish Biography*) have been referred to in the text, those listed below were the main sources consulted for purposes of this publication.

Books:

Chuinneagáin, Síle, *Catherine Mahon, First Woman President of the INTO*, Dublin: INTO, 1998.

Devine, Francis and Smethurst, John B, *Historical Directory of Trade Unions in Ireland*, Dublin: Irish Labour History Society and Working Class Movement Library, 2017.

O'Connell, TJ, *100 Years of Progress, The Story of the Irish National Teachers' Organisation*, Dublin: INTO, 1968.

Puirséil, Niamh, *Kindling the Flame, 150 Years of the Irish National Teachers' Organisation*, Dublin: Gill Books, 2017.

Publications, including Union Journals and Reports:

INTO Journals viz. *Irish School Weekly (1905-1955), An Múinteoir Náisiúnta (1956-1984), Tuarascáil (1979-1997), InTouch (1997+)*.

Annual Reports of the INTO CEC (Central Executive Committee).

Guide to Annual Congress (of INTO).

Annual Directories (INTO).

Newspapers (National and Local) via the *Irish Newspaper Archive*.

Irish Trade Union Congress (ITUC) Annual Reports via website of the Irish Labour History Society.

Photograph on back cover:

A fully-captioned copy of this 1951 photograph – with details of those present who became president updated to 1968 – was published in the INTO journal *An Múinteoir Náisiúnta*, October 1971, p.24.